The Arctic Ocean

by Anne Ylvisaker

Consultant:
Sarah E. Schoedinger
Education Coordinator
Consortium for Oceanographic Research and Education
Washington, D.C.

Bridgestone Books
an imprint of Capstone Press
Mankato, Minnesota

Bridgestone Books are published by Capstone Press
151 Good Counsel Drive, P.O. Box 669, Mankato, Minnesota 56002
http://www.capstone-press.com

Library of Congress Cataloging-in-Publication Data
Ylvisaker, Anne.
    The Arctic Ocean / by Anne Ylvisaker.
    p. cm.—(Oceans)
    Includes bibliographical references and index.
    Summary: Introduces the earth's smallest ocean, and provides instructions for an
activity to demonstrate how ice floats.
    ISBN 0-7368-1423-X (hardcover)
    1. Oceanography—Arctic Ocean—Juvenile literature. [1. Arctic Ocean.
2. Oceanography.] I. Title.
GC401 .Y58 2003
551.46'8—dc21   2001007907

Editorial Credits

Megan Schoeneberger, editor; Karen Risch, product planning editor; Linda Clavel,
    designer; Image Select International, photo researcher

Photo Credits

Andrew Syred/Science Photo Library, 18; Art Directors and TRIP/A. Kuznetsov, 8
(photo); Art Directors and TRIP/B. Crenshaw, 4; Art Directors and TRIP/H. Rogers,
20; Digital Wisdom/Mountain High, 6, 8 (map); Erin Scott/SARIN Creative, 10;
Eyewire, cover, 16; ImageState, 12; PhotoDisc, Inc., 14; RubberBall Productions, 22, 23

1 2 3 4 5 6 07 06 05 04 03 02

Table of Contents

The Arctic Ocean

The Arctic Ocean is the smallest ocean. It covers more than 3 million square miles (8 million square kilometers). The Arctic Ocean is slightly smaller than one and one-half times the size of the United States.

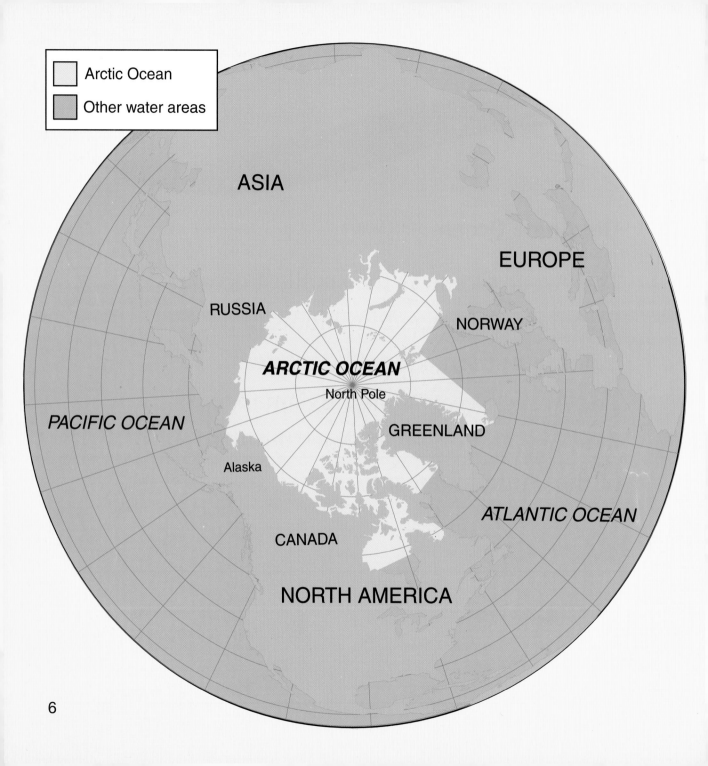

Arctic Ocean
Other water areas

ASIA

EUROPE

RUSSIA

NORWAY

ARCTIC OCEAN

North Pole

PACIFIC OCEAN

GREENLAND

Alaska

ATLANTIC OCEAN

CANADA

NORTH AMERICA

The Location of the Arctic Ocean

The Arctic Ocean lies north of Asia, Europe, and North America. Norway and Russia border one side of the Arctic Ocean. Canada, Greenland, and Alaska border the other side. The North Pole is in the middle of the Arctic Ocean.

North Pole
the most northern point on Earth

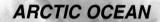

ARCTIC OCEAN   ← Svalbard

North Pole •

Ocean Depths

deepest   shallowest

The Arctic Ocean is covered with ice and icebergs. Icebergs are large pieces of floating ice. Scientists use ships called icebreakers to move through the ice. They then can study different parts of the ocean.

8

The Depth of the Arctic Ocean

The average depth of the Arctic Ocean is 8,189 feet (2,496 meters). The deepest place in the Arctic Ocean lies slightly north of the islands of Svalbard. There, the Arctic Ocean is more than 3 miles (4.8 kilometers) deep.

depth
a measure of how deep something is

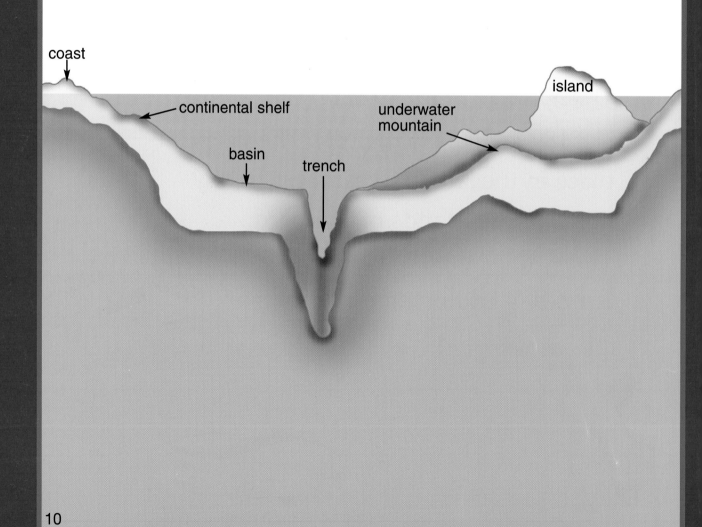

coast

continental shelf

basin

trench

underwater mountain

island

10

The Bottom of the Arctic Ocean

Much of the Arctic Ocean's floor is shallow. The continental shelf slopes from the ocean's shores down to the basin. The basin has mountains and trenches. The Lomonosov Ridge is the tallest mountain range in the Arctic Ocean.

basin
the low, flat part
of an ocean's floor

The Water in the Arctic Ocean

Arctic water is cold and salty. The water near the surface has the least amount of salt. The water near the ocean floor has the most salt. Average surface water temperatures are less than 29 degrees Fahrenheit (1.5 degrees Celsius below zero).

surface
the top or outside layer of something

Fun Fact
Earth leans away from the sun during winter. The sun does not rise in the Arctic region for parts of January and February. Earth leans toward the sun during summer. The Arctic region then has sunlight all day and all night.

The Climate around the Arctic Ocean

Much of the Arctic Ocean is covered with ice. Some of the ice is frozen seawater called sea ice. The rest of the ice is glacier ice. The air above the ocean is cold and dry. Only a small amount of rain or snow falls. Air near the coast sometimes is foggy during summer.

glacier ice
frozen fresh water

Fun Fact
Large icebergs are called ice islands. Scientists have set up research stations on some thick ice islands.

16

Animals in the Arctic Ocean

Arctic animals can live in very cold weather. Puffins and other birds live on Arctic islands. Walruses and polar bears spend time on land and in the water. Whales come to feed in the Arctic Ocean during summer. Fish such as cod and halibut swim in the Arctic Ocean.

halibut
a type of fish used for food

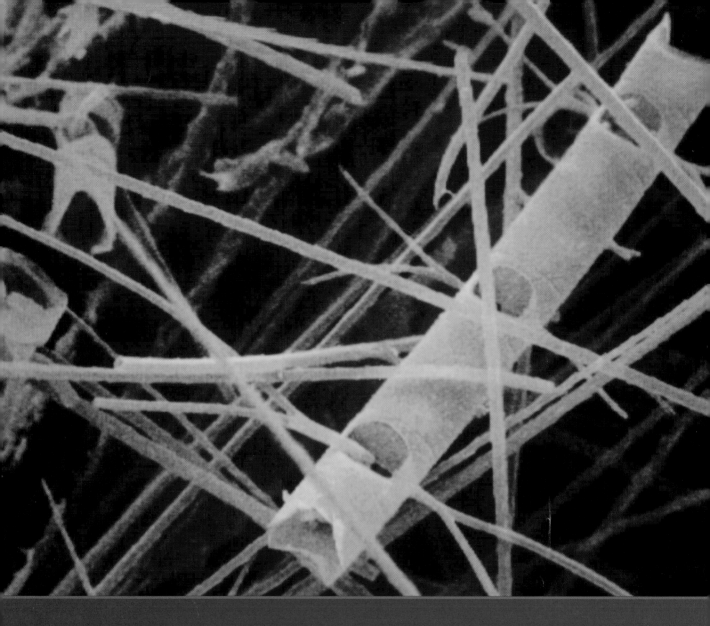

This photo of phytoplankton was taken through a microscope. A microscope makes very small objects appear large enough to study.

Plants in the Arctic Ocean

The Arctic Ocean has few plants. Most plants do not grow well in cold and dark areas. Some tiny plants called phytoplankton float near the surface of the Arctic Ocean. Phytoplankton need the spring and summer sun to grow. Some phytoplankton grow in the sea ice.

Fun Fact
A fulmar is a type of bird that lives on rocky shores. This fulmar has been affected by an oil spill. A healthy fulmar has bright white and gray feathers.

Keeping the Arctic Ocean Healthy

People are working to keep the Arctic Ocean clean. Ships have spilled oil into the Arctic Ocean. Oil can kill plants and animals. It sticks to the feathers of birds. People sometimes hunt and fish in the Arctic Ocean. Too much fishing and hunting also can hurt Arctic wildlife.

Hands On: How Ice Floats

Much of the Arctic Ocean is covered with ice. Icebergs are large pieces of floating ice. You can see the top of an iceberg from a ship. But the largest part of the iceberg is under water. Try this activity to see how ice floats.

What You Need

Paper cup
Freezer
Water
Clear plastic bowl

What You Do

1. Fill a paper cup a little more than half full with water. Put it in the freezer. Wait until the water is frozen.
2. Fill the bowl more than halfway with water.
3. Peel the paper cup away from the ice.
4. Slide the ice into the bowl.
5. Look to see how much of the ice is above the water and how much is below.

Ice floats because it is lighter than water. But some of the ice stays below the water's surface.

Words to Know

average (AV-uh-rij)—the most common amount of something; an average amount is found by adding figures together and dividing by the number of figures.

climate (KLEYE-muht)—the usual weather that occurs in a place

cod (KOD)—a fish with white meat that some people eat

continental shelf (KON-tuh-nuhn-tuhl SHELF)—the shallow area of an ocean's floor near a coast

phytoplankton (FITE-oh-plangk-tuhn)—tiny plants that drift in oceans; phytoplankton are too small to be seen without a microscope.

puffin (PUF-uhn)—a black and white seabird with a colorful beak

trench (TRENCH)—a long, narrow valley in an ocean

Read More

Butterfield, Moira. *Arctic.* Where Am I? Mankato, Minn.: Thameside Press, 1999.

Penny, Malcolm. *The Polar Seas.* Seas and Oceans. Austin, Texas: Raintree Steck-Vaughn, 1997.

Prevost, John F. *Arctic Ocean.* Oceans and Seas. Minneapolis: Abdo Publishing Company, 2000.

Internet Sites

Animals of the Arctic
http://tqjunior.thinkquest.org/3500
Oceanlink
http://www.oceanlink.island.net

Index